William Bolcom

Suites No. 1 and No. 2 for Solo Violin

Corrected Edition

ISBN 978-1-4950-2506-8

EXCLUSIVELY DISTRIBUTED BY

HAL•LEONARD® CORPORATION

7777 W. BLUEMOUND RD. P.O. BOX 13819 MILWAUKEE, WI 53213

www.ebmarks.com
www.halleonard.com

PERFORMANCE NOTES

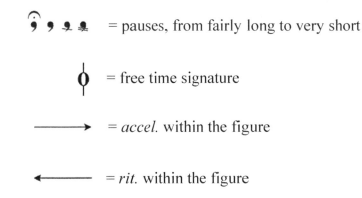

= pauses, from fairly long to very short

= free time signature

= *accel.* within the figure

= *rit.* within the figure

Accidentals obtain throughout a beamed group. Unbeamed notes continue the same accidental until interrupted by another note or rest. (Additional courtesy accidentals are given to ensure clarity.) In music with key signatures, traditional rules apply.

Suite No. 1, although composed in 1977, was premiered by Sergiu Luca at the Cascade Head Festival on June 7, 1987 at the Sitka Center for Art & Ecology in Otis, Oregon. It was first recorded by Philip Ficsor on the CD *American Double - The Bolcom Project* on Albany Records [Troy959/60] in 2007.

Suite No. 2 was commissioned by Music Accord for Gil Shaham, who gave the premiere on February 5, 2013 at the Wheeler Opera House in Aspen, Colorado in the opening concert of the Aspen Music Festival's Winter Music series, 2013.

William Bolcom

Suite No. 1
for Solo Violin

1. Prelude
2. Perpetuum mobile
3. Valse obsédée
4. Sarabande
5. Presto possibile

in memory of Sergiu Luca

Suite No. 1

for solo violin

WILLIAM BOLCOM
(1977)

1. Prelude

* i.e., as <u>bow</u> <u>travels</u>, let it "bounce"

Just fast enough; strict time

As before

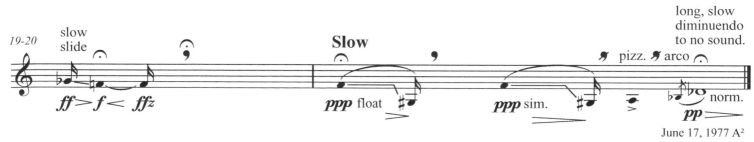

June 17, 1977 A²

*The 32nds are grouped in 4's, with barlines every fourth "beat," for ease of reading only. No beat is implied.

2. Perpetuum mobile

Fast; even 16ths throughout (<u>not</u> Prestissimo)

♩ = c. 102

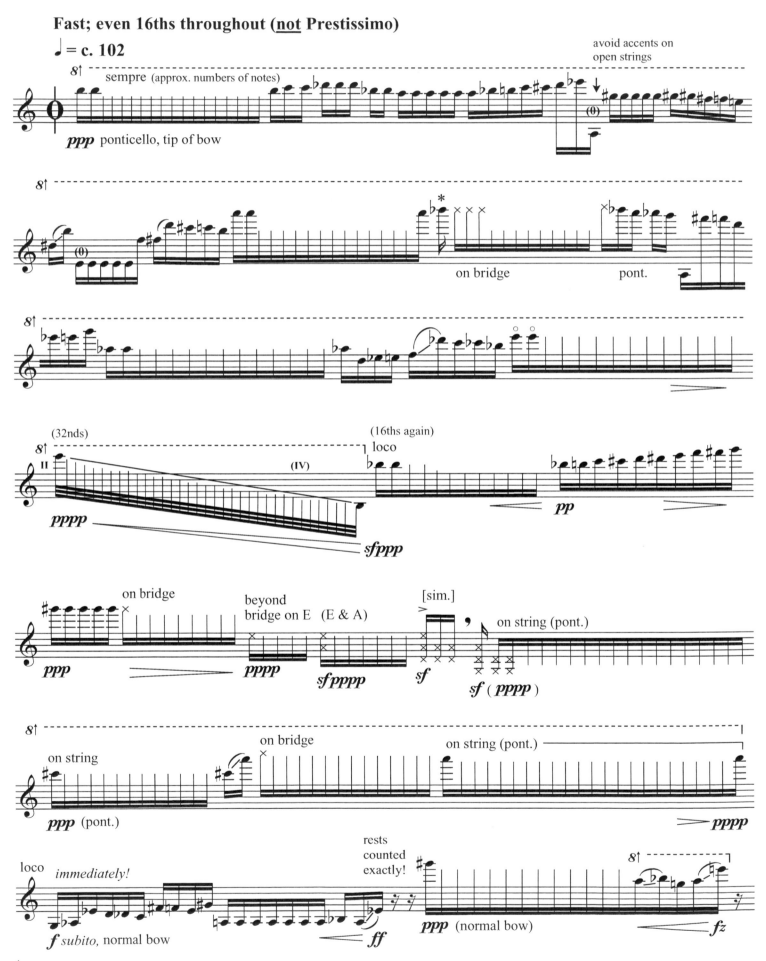

* At this and similar places, keep previous stopped note.

* bow <u>and</u> fingerings beyond bridge.

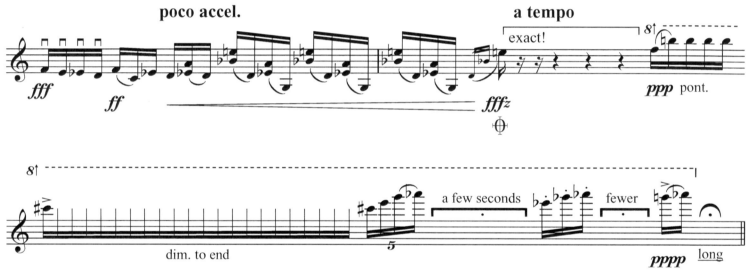

Aug. 13, '77 A²

segue

(blank for page turn)

3. Valse obsédée

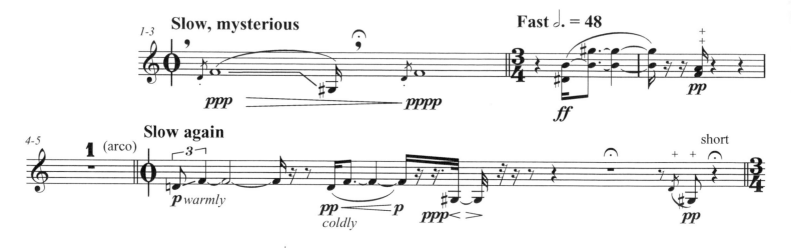

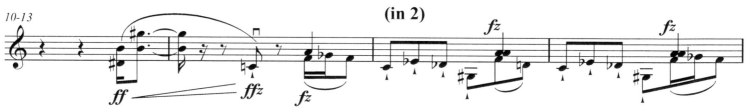

keep tempo, exactly to end

(exact)

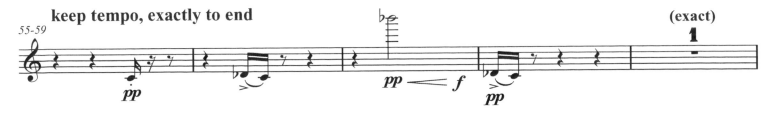

Aug. 17, '77 A[2]

(blank for page turn)

14

4. Sarabande

Not too slow ♩ = **36-40**

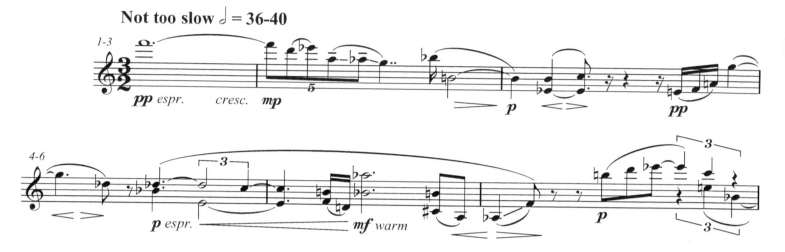

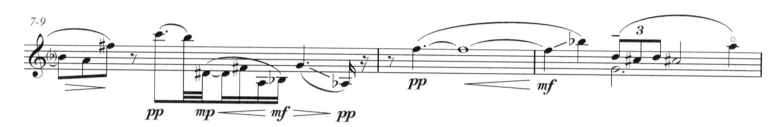

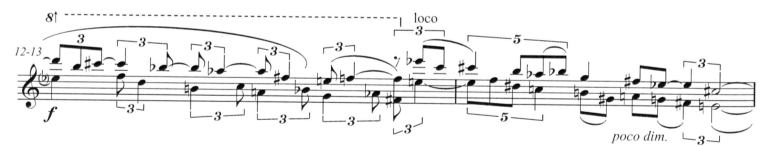

20-22

23-24
non harm.

25-27

28-30

31-32

33-34

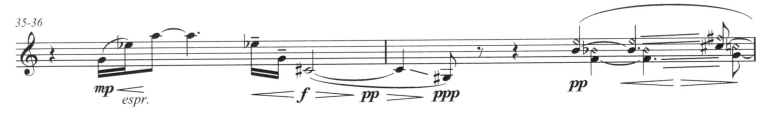

35-36

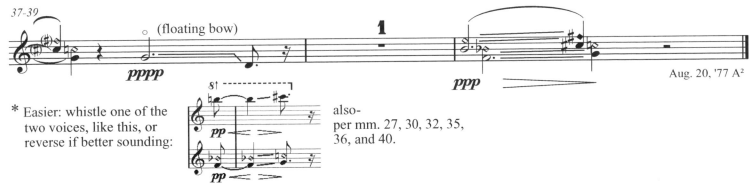

37-39

(floating bow)

Aug. 20, '77 A²

* Easier: whistle one of the
two voices, like this, or
reverse if better sounding:

also-
per mm. 27, 30, 32, 35,
36, and 40.

5. Presto possibile

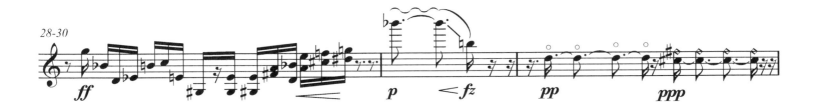

V. S.

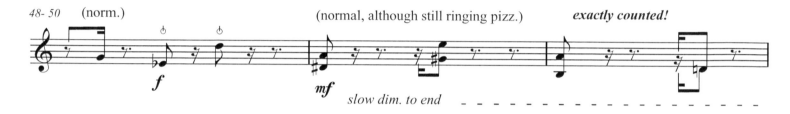

Aug. 24, '77 A²

Suite No. 2
for Solo Violin

1. Morning music
2. Dancing in place
3. Northern Nigun
4. Lenny in spats
5. Tempo di gavotte
6. Barcarolle
7. Fuga malinconica
8. Tarantella
9. Evening music

Commissioned for Gil Shaham by Music Accord

Suite No. 2
for solo violin

WILLIAM BOLCOM
(2011)

1. Morning music

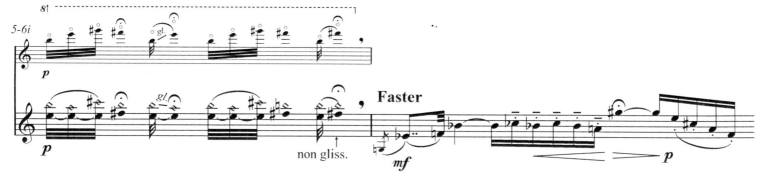

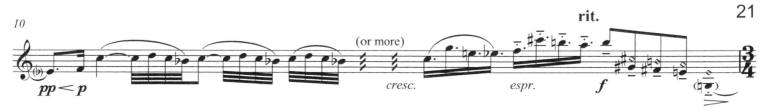

Sarabande tempo

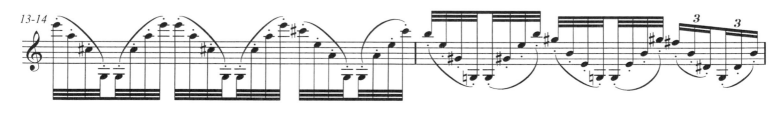

slow   **slower**

3/30/11 rev. 4/14
A² - NYC

2. Dancing in place

x = fingerboard notes

* fingerboard notes: hit fingerboard with end
  of left hand finger to produce a note.

25-28

< f

(l. h. pizz.) +   +

ff

29-31

f   *mp*   *cresc.*   *f < ffz*

gliss.

32-34

hold steady!

mf   *ffz*   *mp*

x   x   x   x   x   x

* f. n. _____

35-38   *sfz*   **non rit.**

ff   *p*   *p*   *p*

x   x   x   x   x   x   f. n.   x   x   x   x   x

f. n. _____

pp

segue

4/13/11
NYC

* fingerboard notes

24

3. Northern Nigun

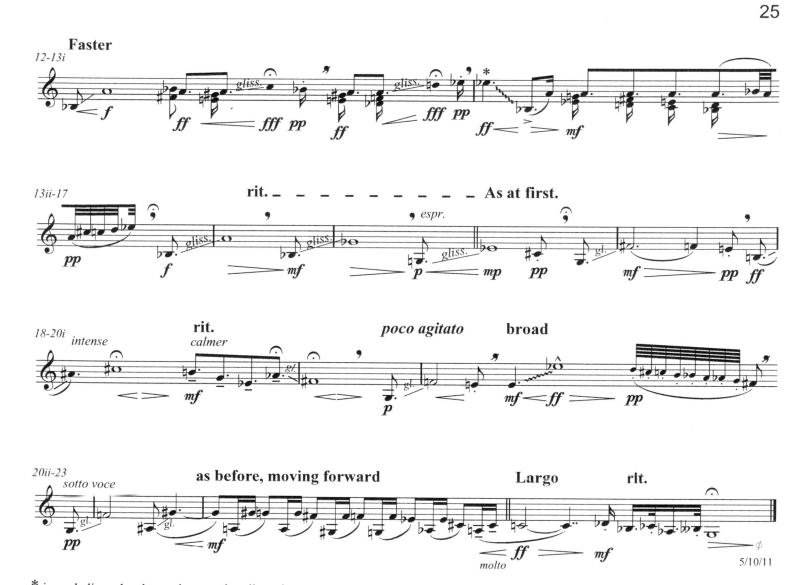

* jagged glissando: slower than regular glissando.

for Jamie
(à la mémoire de guess who)

4. Lenny in spats

5/19/11 A²

(blank for turn)

5. Tempo di gavotte

5/24/11 A²

6. Barcarolle

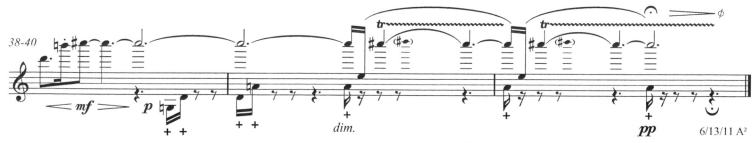

7. Fuga malinconica

5/31/11

(Blank for page turn)

8. Tarantella

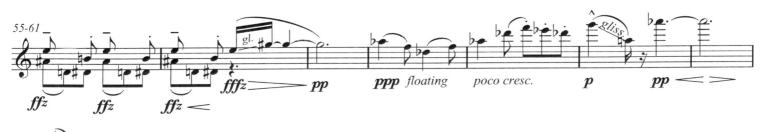

6/16/11 A²

Finale:
9. Evening music

*slow gliss.

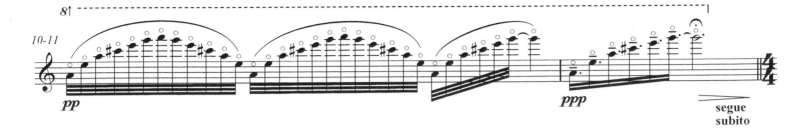

Coda:

♩ = 76 **Duettini**

a tempo
sotto voce al fine

6/18/11 A²